YOUR MINDSET, YOUR EVERYTHING

J S WEY

1

It has taken me a good deal of strength, confidence and willpower to get to where I am today. However, I am writing my story, not because I am looking for sympathy or even understanding. Nor am I searching for a way out of the darkness into which I found myself heading, becoming darker and bleaker with each step I took.

That darkness happened a while ago, when I stepped into a bank of grey cloud. Little did I know that this would transform me and almost overwhelm me. Almost, but not quite. It didn't swallow me up and destroy me, as some might have expected. I emerged into the light. I gained strength from suffering. I may have emerged badly bruised and hurting, but I found I could still smile and I could still laugh and sing. I could still be me. What more can anyone ask?

The real reason I have written this book and want people to read it is because I want it to be for others. I want to reach out to all of those people who have suffered and perhaps are still suffering, even if their pain is not on the same wavelength as mine. They will have travelled a different path, seen, heard and felt different things. Experiences may be similar but never the same. There are many books out there, and each time you read someone else's story you come across something, maybe just a line or two, telling you something new. It is this that enriches us all.

I hope to inspire and uplift the reader; I hope more than anything to help people to see how they, too, will one day be able to smile again, and to laugh and sing with the birds. I want you to believe in yourself.

It can happen.

It will happen.

Anyone can make it happen. Just as I made it happen.

Let me now go back to when my daughter was a young girl, but mature enough to be told what I was about to tell her; she was about to learn some life truths from her mother. I sat her down and told her my story.

"I want you to know," I began, "of the way I learned my skills of survival."

She looked at me a little surprised, her deep brown eyes questioning but nonetheless ready to listen.

I wanted to give her my knowledge, and to arm her against any difficulty or misfortune that might come her way. It was a gift I wanted to give, the best a mother could do. Her mind is her life, for her to be in charge of and not anyone else.

"I did not learn in the way that others learn to enjoy sipping a cup of coffee in times of crisis or stress, or enjoy hot, soothing tea," I said.

I could understand her confused expression. To her, at that point, I must have been talking gibberish. This didn't worry me. I thought I actually had quite a lot of mumbo jumbo in me to gibber about.

"Those things that conjure up images of warmth, comfort and conviviality are natural home comforts," I said, "the kind we all expect to come our way from time to time."

I looked at her smooth, blemish-free, dark brown skin. So young, so innocent, so far removed from the world I had inhabited. It was this that made me so determined that she would not suffer in the same way, or experience what I had.

"You see," I said, "in a manner of speaking, your hands will be clasped securely around your mug of tea or coffee, never wanting to let go."

My daughter listened to my words in quiet anticipation. She clearly had no idea what I was on about. I wasn't even sure, to be honest, whether I did either. Still, I was beginning to feel more confident now that I knew that I held her attention and she wasn't going to run away in fright. I had been worried she might think her mother had freaked out. She could have been forgiven for thinking that she was about to go the same way too.

"The feeling of holding that warm vessel of liquid," I said, by now in full flow, "is comforting. It warms the heart. It relaxes small and vulnerable fingers too, and has the simple ability of making life so enjoyable."

She stared at me with her warm, chocolate-brown eyes. She looked almost transfixed.

I was on a roll. I was beginning to enjoy myself. I thought I could be quite good at this sort of stuff, given time and a bit of extra know-how.

"But it wasn't like that for me," I said, a bit worried my voice might have sounded like a blunt hammer.

She twisted her fingers in her lap. I could see she wanted to hear more but was understandably nervous of what might follow. I could hardly blame her.

I ploughed on, regardless. "It was a move away from reality," I said, unsure now whether the hammer had turned into an axe. "It was a hard knock that no child should have to bear."

She blinked and held her 5' 5" slim frame very still.

"What happened to me came like a shock," I said, "a force of something unpleasant which I could not control."

She nodded.

I felt in that tiny movement of her head that she had shown understanding, a raw and uncanny knowledge that this was serious. It was also something which might be worth listening to. Her mother wasn't quite so mad after all. She relaxed her features visibly, her lovely brown eyes showing a new depth of meaning. Her shoulders looked less tense and stiff, her hands untwisted.

"And the events in my life," I said, "landed on me like a missile."

I had no need to say more. It was as if she had grown. She sat before me, thoughtful, a slight shake of her head… and wanting to know more.

Well, it is said that a strong, confident woman has power that is unimaginable. Yes, of course, it is easy to read words or to hear wonderful expressions, to nod and agree with the sentiment. You think how true they are, understanding the inherent message that lies within the words, making you feel in that moment, strong, joyous, capable.

Then the words drift away. Like a fleeting mist, like the sun that shines and then disappears behind thick cloud for the rest of the day, the words vanish in the air. Gone. Then it is as if you never read or heard those words, so fleeting was their effect.

You sink back to your misery… and to your fear. Nothing works. You are the same person as you were before you read those words.

But wait…

My words, in this book, are different. They tell a story, real and alive. The words in this book will tell you my story. Just as I gave my daughter the gift of knowing my story and the vital elements of survival I learned from it, so too I give my gift to those who read this book, my powerful strength, my strong confidence. This is all the richer because it comes from the heart of a young girl who once had no such riches, a girl without strength, with no power and devoid of confidence.

That girl is me. I learned how to use every problem I faced as a stepping-stone to the next level in my life. The problems became positive instead of negative. I didn't sink or become overwhelmed by difficulty. I saw barriers as a chance to leap to a new level, instead of a crushing obstacle.

How?

I know that is the burning question and one to which you will be eager to know the answer. However, I don't just give you the answer, I help you to *learn* the answer. Because I am helping you to be you. I want you not just to overcome your barriers, but to leap over them like hurdles and transform yourself.

To begin with, for me, and I suspect for many others, fear was the key. For everyone, this will loom up in different ways. Fear is a wonderful key. Use its power, don't waste it. Draw on its unending strength. It will give back more than you could wish for, not its negative force for that is nothing, simply wind. It will throw back all the positive energy stored inside its mighty weight.

I knew instinctively, from an early age, that I would have to learn how to conquer fear if I wanted to succeed. I learned it at that age when fingers are clasped around warmth, when security is transposed to the joy of being alive, to the energy, youth and vigour that fills a developing, young mind.

My mind, like the smooth unblemished fingers of my youth, felt as if it had been dipped in a big pond of fear. I was ruled by it.

Yet, slowly, inexorably, I began to see that fear is nothing. It appears to hold you in its grip. It likes to be something for you to honour, to be in awe of its magnificent hold, its smiling features and its pleasure at being by your side, day and night.

How easy it is to be deluded, to be sucked into its embrace, to feel it replacing the warm coffee or the soothing golden tea. It loves to control you.

When the day comes when you begin to see just how much fear likes to dominate and control, often in a teasing way, it beckons and by now you have no option but to follow. It laughs, you cower. You try a raw, tentative, nervous smile because you're trying, really trying, to do your best.

It leads you ever forward into false security. Like stepping into quicksand, smiling and waving at everyone… without realising the danger that awaits you in that quicksand. The danger of being swallowed alive.

Fear, I began to realise, is a mental state. It can be changed. There is no fear. There is only the air that you breathe, and which keeps you alive. That is the real smile, the real laughter. That, too, is the real power, full of rich earth and density, full of everything that makes life worth living.

When you live in freedom, you feel this, and it is powerful. When you are in prison, you don't feel it, you are controlled by others, and your every action is observed and recorded.

Fear can hold you prisoner, in a dank, uncomfortable prison cell with its plain grey walls, its distinct smell and nameless faces. Keys jangling, no hope of escape.

It was not that I reached forward and snatched those prison keys away from this thing that gripped me so hard, this thing that threatened with its smiling, friendly features to destroy me. It was simply that I wasn't going to let it drag me into that stifling cell at the outset. Because if I had, I knew I would be finished.

We fear rejection.

We fear failure.

We fear how people perceive us.

We fear speaking the truth.

We fear just being ourselves.

What if we didn't have fear?

I decided that this was how I was going to live, without fear. I was not about to be its victim.

We all have a starting point to our fears. As a child, you start being afraid of things because of the experiences you have had, but you do not know how they are affecting you, you're too young; you think that is life and how it should be, there is nothing else. This is how my fears started, from childhood experiences.

We were living on the beautiful South African west coast, on the Western Cape. This area is like a discovery, it is full of beaches in their wild, natural beauty, unspoilt by the ravages of tourism. In spring, the wild flowers in this region lay a wonderful carpet of colour across the land. Apart from Route 27, the main holiday highway heading out of Capetown, this place could be miles from anywhere, a blank absence on the glossy pages of the holiday brochures.

Except that this route is a seafood haven. Open-air beach restaurants abound on this stretch and offer delicious seafood which has been freshly caught from the sea. It is cooked on open fires with the glorious sunset offering a superlative backdrop.

I sat with my daughter on one of these beaches, by our seaside holiday home.

"Just look at the sunset," I said to her, raising my eyes to the distance. The waves, just in front of where we sat, glided and rolled onto the beach.

"It looks like the sun is really sinking into the sea," she said, following my gaze.

"Yes, you're right," I said. "The air is so still, isn't it?"

Her dark, curly black hair glinted in the last rays of the sun, adding a luxurious shine to it.

"I know what you mean," she said, "it's like it has a special evening glow."

I laughed. "And only a sun sinking into the distance of the sea can create that," I said, transfixed by the crimson stretch, gracing the horizon above the coastline.

In the background, the mountain range of the Cederberg Mountains was simply stunning. I loved to gaze at their majestic wonder, in awe at their magnificence that defied description.

"Look," my daughter pointed to the sea, "just look how those rays have cast a red-gold streak across the sea. It dazzles."

There we sat, mesmerised into a quiet spiritual togetherness, by the natural beauty that confronted us, so unadulterated by human forces.

"You know something," I said to her. "What we see before us is a daily ritual performed with such ease."

As we sat there, gazing out to sea, the sun gradually lowering in the sky, it was as if there was a sudden change in the atmosphere.

We both felt it, I know.

Along this stretch of the coast, from Cape Town to the border with the Northern Cape at Touws River, there were small historic towns and fishing villages, picture-book quaint and at ease with their location.

Snoek, mussels and crayfish can be found in abundance here, creating a way of life for the inhabitants. Salted mullet – or bokkums – are strung up in bunches and left to dry, a renowned local delicacy. It spelled out a message. Of hope and something more, of simplicity and survival.

This seemed so symbolic of the way this sudden shift in the air had happened between us as we sat there. It was a reminder of good healthy living and of being amongst fellow people who belonged to a community. It was the balanced order of things, a sign that things were fine, everything would turn out all right.

There was also an expectation. This came with a feeling of release. In sitting here with my daughter, surrounded by so much that was wholesome and good, a message was being strung out.

I began to break the silence, to talk to her and allow the release to unfold. I knew she would listen.

I turned my head towards her.

"You know," I said, "there are so many truths that I have hidden deep inside me for so long."

She turned her face, her rich brown eyes searching mine. For a few still seconds our eyes were locked together. Here was a bond that could not be broken, only strengthened.

My voice came out in barely a whisper.

"The truths that led to my fears and my insecurities," I said, "nearly destroyed me."

In the background the ebb and flow of the sea rustled and swished onto the sand. A golden, wonderful silence of delightful noise. It was indescribable. Still, the sun sank lower, as if measuring my every word.

"Until," I continued, my voice soft, no longer a whisper, but gaining strength in a synonymous twist with what I was saying and the atmosphere in which we sat, "until I took control of my mental state."

There was a very fine breeze coming in from the sea; it carried with it the taste of something fresh, not bitter.

She looked at her feet; they were clad in her favourite

leather sandals, a little worn but with the comfort of years, like an old cardigan you don't want to part with, even though it has gathered holes.

"I began to realise," I said, "that there were things I had long ago suppressed. They lay buried deep in my soul, wanting to be forgotten, yet so full of voice."

She took her eyes off her feet and looked out to sea.

Still that wonderful unspoken bond of love and life persisted, throbbing between us, almost tangible in the crisp, salty air.

"They were things that I now realise lay buried beneath the layers of life that had passed me by," I said, my voice gaining increasing strength. "Perhaps they had been crying out for release for a very long time and I had ignored their plea to be released into the wild. I have stamped down on them until now, even more fiercely, determined not to allow them to bother me. I have done the exact opposite of what I should have done. I should have listened to their screams, dragged them out and taken a firm grip on them. I should have confronted them, instead of thinking I could banish them by pushing them further down inside me."

I tapped my foot on the sandy ground beneath. The sun had reached the horizon, just touching it on its lower rim, on its way to the dawn of a morning somewhere else. In these moments of quiet, I knew that now was the time for the voice of these suppressed emotions to be heard, to come tumbling out into the open world. They had finally found a route out.

I spoke candidly, without the stiff tension of someone forcing their words, unsure whether to hold back or continue. I told her how having faith in God and in myself had helped me to develop my confidence and lose all sense of fear. These were the elements that had become my pillar, holding me up in times of struggle and challenge. They had become my survival tools, what I leaned on when I needed intrinsic strength, and fortitude at my own command. It is this, I was certain, that had led to my recovery.

2

———

"I was born into a Roman Catholic Family," I began. My father, William, was once a priest and met my mother, Maria, by chance, on the very morning he had decided that this would be the day he ended his priesthood. I do not know the full story of my parents' meeting, and have only been able to piece some facts together from my mother's diary.

It was a bright Sunday morning when he had just finished his morning prayers. He sat alone, deep in thought. He had joined the seminary at the tender age of 16. Now, at 26, he was a robust young man, an adult in his prime, but all he had known of life, since 16, was the life of a priest. He was a virgin. He had never known what it felt like to be with a woman, to enjoy romance, longing and togetherness, to be loved, other than by God. The thought of leaving the seminary had been on his mind for a long time though, and as he sat there looking at the Cross of Jesus in front of him, it was then that he said his last prayer as a priest.

On the other side of the same small village, my mother, Maria, was blossoming from a young girl into a fine young woman. Her parents – my grandparents – wanted to marry her off as quickly as possible. This was the custom for women of her age, done like posting a parcel into a pillar box. However, Maria had other ideas. She was a stubborn young woman and, out of all her siblings, she had a mind of her own. She had decided that she was not yet ready to meet a convenient match and settle down to quiet domestic marriage, doing her duty. She was adamant. No one was going to make her get married. My mother had resolutely set her mind on experiencing more of what life was about, and of tasting the finer things life had to offer. Little did she know that her dreams were about to be cut short, like scissors slicing through a clean sheet of paper. All hope of going back to her original state was to be lost.

On a bright sunny morning, William was woken by the melodic sound of birds singing in the trees, charming, bright and piercingly shrill at times. This, he remembered, was to be his first morning away from the priesthood, and so far it looked as if a positive day was dawning, ready for him to embrace a new life; but of just how new a life, he had no idea at that point. He rose from his bed, showered, dressed, and feeling fresh and invigorated with the promise of the day he made his way to his local church for the usual morning prayers. Only this time he was not the priest, just an ordinary member of the village congregation.

Maria also arrived that morning at the church, with a new era stretching ahead of her. In the bright sparkling sunlight, bouncing off the Church spire, the day looked to be a good one.

In the church, William and Maria were introduced to one another. They immediately felt attracted to each other. However, William then moved away from the village because he needed to find a new career. Being a priest was all he had ever known. He had no idea what path he would like to take, but he knew that whatever path he took it involved helping others.

Several years later, on another of those fine, sunny mornings that are so full of promise, quite by chance, William bumped into Maria again. Unbeknown to him, she had moved to the same city, Sun City, South Africa, to find a job after graduating as a nurse. She had just been for an interview at the same hospital where William worked.

"Maria," he called out when he spotted her, "what a lovely surprise."

"Indeed, it has been a couple of years since I last saw you," she replied. Then she added with a note of fun, "Are you a midwife?" This was a joke often used in Africa at the time, because in Africa in those days male nurses were laughed at, in much the same way they were in the United Kingdom. The culture considered nursing to be a woman's job, a thing that only women could do, and this was why she said this.

"Not at all," he responded, "I am on the medical panel of the hospital. I was asked to fill in for a colleague who could not attend at the last minute." William had qualified as a general doctor a few years back.

That was the beginning and the rest is history. They married a year later.

Just like Maria, William had the idea of owning a practice in his home town. After a few years of working in the city, and earning enough to start their own practice, they relocated back to their village where they started a small practice and set up a few small businesses.

They became very prominent members of the village community. They had wealth and were well-known around the village. As time passed, they eventually started a family. They had 7 children, and I was the unexpected 7th child. This was because Maria, my mother, was nearly menopausal when she had me.

I was born in Gabane, a small village in Botswana, on the outskirts of the capital, Gaborone. This serves as the seat of government of Botswana, and is located about 15 kilometres from Botswana's border with South Africa, in south-east Botswana. Before gaining independence in 1966, this was one of the poorest and least-developed states in the world. By the time I was born, my siblings were grown men and women, with their own children. I therefore did not have the same upbringing as my siblings, and had no strong relationship with most of them.

I did not actually grow up with my parents and nor do I know much about their history. I was sort of an accidental child, born to them at an older age, albeit loved, and hence my name Keitumetse, which means Joy. When I reached the age of 4, I was sent to live with my older brother in neighbouring South Africa. My mother believed that growing up in a developing city would equip me better than staying with her in the village. Having said that, my mother still lived a comfortable life in the village and, perhaps with what happened over the coming years, it is testimony to the fact that achievement and riches cannot replace a mother's physical presence and love, and the special bond that goes with it. For me that bond was absent. In effect, when the umbilical cord is cut a baby's life support is also cut; for most children this is immediately replaced by natural air, with still the mother's bond being there. However, in my case, my mother's bond had been snatched cruelly away. Little did my mother know this at the time, or that she had sent her daughter to a life that would haunt her for ever. From that time on, I never saw my parents again, until I was in my twenties.

The problem I immediately faced, in my new home, was that my sister-in-law – my brother's wife – did not like me that much. I felt alone growing up. I had no one to lean on and to whom I could turn for support. Probably as a result, I was a very quiet child and isolated, with no real friends. If I needed anything, I had to ask my brother, who became a rough substitute for my mum and dad. My brother was also a very strict man. Everything we did was watched closely. Life with his family continued as normal; well, as normal it could be. I was a much-loved, last born of the family, albeit split apart from my mum and dad. I was growing up with my nephews and nieces, so I was a lot closer to them than to my own brothers and sisters.

I started school, and began to grow up into a beautiful young girl. By the time I was aged 11, I had become very smart and capable. As my sister-in-law had not treated me well since I first arrived, I'd had to quickly learn to fend for myself; find ways of getting pocket money through doing favours for the older children. In Africa, we did not have washing machines at the time, therefore washing a pair of jeans meant hard labour. To this day most families still do not have the luxury of washing machines or hoovers. I would offer to wash all my older nieces' and nephews' clothes to earn the pennies.

"Hey, you know how it is," I told one of nieces, who was my favourite customer. "Shirts are light therefore one shilling, khaki and jeans require scrubbing therefore five shillings per two pairs," I said.

We also took turns to cook for the whole large family, which comprised both my immediate and extended family. We had days when the meal was flat bread and stew. As a rule everyone had to be given four flat breads, which meant making eighty flat breads plus extras, because the older boys would steal some while we were cooking. This too was a source of income because no one wanted to cook that many flat breads, so I would offer to cook them in exchange for a fee. These were fun times.

It was when I was approaching the age of 12 that my life started to take a dramatic turn for the worse. I started getting sexual abuse.

I started being repeatedly sexually abused by a relative who was about 35 years older than me. He had seven children of his own, some of whom were also abused by him. Owing to their feelings of shame, a common emotion amongst victims of abuse is that they prefer to leave everything hidden and not refer to the abuse they suffered. If they could, I know they would tell their own stories, but the shame surrounding this kind of thing is not easy to face.

To begin with, you must be in a good place in your mind. You need to be mentally and emotionally balanced enough to take the step of unashamedly revealing what happened as an innocent victim, knowing you are not at fault. I have jumped the barrier and I can look back objectively, but they have not yet got there. They are still in that secret place, and some have children, and they don't want their story revealed to their children, at least not yet or maybe even never.

I am closer to my friends than I am my family, because it is my friends who have been the rock at the most difficult times of my life. It is also significant that the most painful parts of my life have come from blood family. The physical and mental scarring of abuse is immense. You have to have a strong mind to carry and look at these scars.

This relative would ask me to do everything and anything that took his fancy, and which pleased him or gave him a thrill. The abuse went on for several years. By then I had started developing the classic signs of an abused child. I became subdued and silent. I shrank into myself, becoming reserved, keeping everything suppressed inside me, and I lost trust in everyone. To this day, I still lack trust in many people and I am very reserved.

"Mum, you are very reserved, you have a very small circle of people you call friends."

"I've always wanted to ask you how you met dad."

"My dear child, I will tell you later," I laughed. "We have all day and night this is our special day."

We sat in silence for a moment, yet it seemed as though we were still talking; both of us with a little grin on our faces. You could hear the words "I love you" without them being uttered. We had a special bond.

I took a deep breath of that fresh air around us, held on to my daughter's hand and continued while we both stared away into space.

I felt so very alone, in a world that didn't seem to care, I told her; with people who were my family and supposed to be there, to nurture and bring me up in place of my parents, but who took advantage of that trust by abusing me. I had to endure the misery of this abuse, week after week. It went on relentlessly, and there was no one around that I could rely on to help me, no one to trust or get me away from it. The suffering was almost unbearable at times.

Throughout the years that followed, I never knew what it was like to be a normal teenager. I didn't understand the happy balance of discovery, excitement, challenge and care. I only understood tears and fear. It was quite clear, too, that every family member feared him. Yet, despite this, they treated him like a god, in awe of his power. No one would dare stand up to him. I saw through this daily charade, and I could hardly bear it. FEAR, FEAR ,FEAR – that is all I saw in everyone… that is what was in me.

By the time I was 15 years old, I could tolerate the suffering no longer. I tried to commit suicide by taking an overdose of sleeping pills, but I survived the ordeal. I was taken to an emergency department where I received an enema and a wash-out to clear my system. However, little did I know that things were about to get worse.

Everything that happens can scar you physically and emotionally, but I have somehow come through without feeling too scarred. Instead I feel blessed, for I have eliminated fear. I have climbed through the hoops, often ringed with burning flames of fire, but I am safe now. I am safe to tell my story, to save a life if I can, to educate where I can.

One of those hoops was when, at the age of 16, I fell

pregnant from the abuse. When the abuser found out, he made me have an abortion. This is not the sort of abortion where you go to a nice clean clinic and are given hormone injections by professional people who are qualified in medical skills to stop the baby developing, bringing on a natural miscarriage.

This was done by a man who called himself a self-trained doctor… without any qualifications. He was used to this kind of practice, and thought nothing of it. He was used, mainly, by those needing illegal abortions. He carried out his practice in an old building… with very old, unsterile instruments.

I feared for my life. I had no one to turn to for help, no one to whom I could talk and at least release my fear. I had no idea what was going to happen to me, other than something horrible.

The rape which had led to the pregnancy was the action of a pervert. This person was someone whom all the members of my family trusted. He abused this position of trust. He was a very wealthy and well-connected man. It gave him a sense of superiority and of entitlement. I was there for the taking, a pawn, something to be used when it suited him. I was something that could be hidden away and kept quiet after he had abused me. After sexual gratification, I could be dismissed. I was worthless and, as far as he was concerned, it was his right to use my body in this manner.

It wasn't just me. Other young family members were

also subjected to the same sexual abuse. He could pick and choose at will. We were subordinate to him, like playthings, simply there for his pleasure whenever he chose. It all happened between the age of 11 and 16. This is an age when many young girls can feel confused and unsure of themselves, growing into their femininity without knowing what to expect.

When you don't know what is up ahead, and the expectation of what is right is denied you, you have no choice but to conform, to follow the path laid out for you. Most girls of this age are also too young to have independent control of their lives, they are powerless to protest and there is no one out there to whom they can confide, who will listen, take them seriously, and take action. In my case, those around me were in thrall to his power. They knew what was going on. They lived in fear of him, and did whatever he said without objection. Keep quiet and carry on.

As for his wife, well, the fear was even greater. She did not work and had no way of supporting herself. The thought of walking away and leaving her children was unthinkable. She had to bear the pain for the sake of her children, for her own sake in order to survive. She also feared the consequence of what would happen if she ever decided to run away with her children. How would she feed them, where would she start? All these questions seemed to cloud her mind so she just gave in.

He controlled everything. He was a domineering bully. You couldn't get money to buy anything unless you did as he asked. You couldn't go to school unless you followed his orders. You didn't even get money for sanitary pads unless you followed his orders. Yes, it was that bad.

"I am trying to visualise him, Mum, but it still doesn't sink in. How can a relative do this?"

"I wondered the same, my child. I have always wondered and asked myself the same question."

Most people think an abuser is an ugly looking person, a fearful person or strange looking weird person; but in fact I have come to find it is the opposite. This man was a wealthy, good-looking man. Physically, there was nothing to scare anyone. Then how did he control people, one would wonder? It all came down to money. Money is what he used to control everyone. The love of money can make people do things which are unimaginable. There is a saying that money does not change people, it just enhances what is already within. It is true, but it does not mean that the person was just bad and the bad was enhanced.

You see every person has good and bad in them. No one on this earth has only good in them. We all have good and bad, but we have the power to choose to do good or bad. Some will get rich and help others, while some will get rich and harm others. This is a decision made by a person based on their own values. Also, what you feed your mind plays a big role in your day-to-day action. This is why the company you keep also matters. You are more likely to follow the course of the company you keep unless you have a strong mind to know who you are and stand firm in your values regardless of what your companions think. A strong MIND is not easily influenced or manipulated, and this is important in life.

Well, my abuser has now passed on. Yet to this day most of my family members still do not want to bring the subject up and talk about it. It remains a hidden secret. They will simply tell you, "Family matters need to remain in the family." It is complete strangers who have been the people to whom I have turned, when it came to opening up about the ordeal which I endured at his hands.

I am now a mature woman as I write this book, still young and yet with the years sitting on me. After high school, my niece and I were sent away to study in Asia. That is when I was first diagnosed with endometriosis and had surgery, staying in the hospital for four months.

3

My daughter sat there listening as I narrated my story, and I could see in her eyes the burning questions. Pausing her gaze at me, stopping to picture and wonder what could possess your own blood relative to carry out such acts, but she was so keen to hear more, and to know how I managed to stay so strong… I continued with my usual smile that never leaves my face to this day.

I continued with a soft, somehow shaky voice. Well, eventually I told the only people who, I thought, might stand by me and defend me. This included my elder sister; but it had no effect. She carried on like nothing had happened, like nothing was said, like it was normal. She just did not want it ever to be mentioned.

" Bad things happen to good people in this world," she said. "Sometimes you just have to ignore and move on."

"Move on to where? There is nowhere to go," I said

quietly, as though trying to avoid being heard. I mumbled under my breath as I walked away from her. It is customary to have respect for your elders, regardless. You don't respond when they speak. This in many cases led to girls being mistreated, because you had to obey. In our African cultures they confuse respect with silence: when a child speaks, they are considered rude and disrespectful. This has led to many cases of child abuse and neglect, and the corruption in our countries prevents the law being enforced to prevent these crimes. Many perpetrators are not held accountable.

There was still no one who was willing to stand up and put a stop to what was happening. There was no one who was prepared to rescue me, because they were all held in the grip of fear. It was fear of this man, and what he might do. This fear of retribution was too great for anyone to risk their own position and to try to stop him. He held the power, like a ruthless tyrant to whom everyone surrenders, because they are desperate not to be his next victim; they were desperate to cling to him, to be seen to be subservient to his every wish and demand. This sort of behaviour becomes a self-propelling fuel. The more sycophantic they became, the more he loved his control and exerted his dominance. They wanted to win his favour, seeing him as a man of influence. The real irony is that they saw him as a 'protector'. He controlled their minds. They had no mind of their own to make their own choices. People do not realise that someone can influence you, but the final decision is yours if you are in control of your mind.

The pain I endured, whilst under his control, is indescribable. The fear of this man's ruthless and domineering abuse, in the form of sexual bullying, was too great to overcome alone. It kept me captive.

You see, he had this little office… that was the devil's room, as I called it. He went there to work. Alas, it wasn't really work. He kept most of his dark secrets in this room. It was located in our servants' quarter. Most big houses in Africa have servants' quarters. These are little mini-houses that are allocated to helpers to sleep in. Every household, rich or poor, has a maid, unlike in Europe where most people do their own housework. I always wonder how the poor afford to have helpers.

It would all begin by him asking you to go and collect something from his office, or go to the cleaner, or drop off something. He would then follow you and rape you. At times he would tell the family he was taking you to see a doctor, or make up an excuse of some sort for one thing or another and take you to a room somewhere. In Africa, there are many of these sorts of places. You will then do what he required you to do.

"You are so fragile, I have to treat you like a glass, as though you are going to break any minute," he would say. This is because I would cry out for my mother. I would say that I was going to kill myself. I would say that I didn't want live, but somehow I found strength to face another day.

Nearly all our grown-up family members knew what was going on…but it turned out that money spoke louder than truth. The fear of him echoed in every room where you turned.

Yet there was someone to whom I could turn. Someone who would be by my side, day and night, someone who loved me, and always would. It was God, and I found Him.

I started to attend church, and my attendance became very regular. It was my escape. Going off to church was the only time I would be allowed go out, and it was my salvation.

As it happened, this man had grown up in a strong Catholic family, and the belief in attending church had remained with him. He would allow all family members to go to church, although he did not go himself.

It was going to church regularly that started to build my strength. It was, of course, gradual. To begin with, I started having dreams. In the first dream, I saw my abuser – this man – burning in a pot of fire in the sky. He had the devil's horns on his head. I just stood there and looked on. In another dream, a chariot came to rescue me. The man riding the chariot asked me where my pass to heaven was, and I produced my Bible. The man smiled, and the chariot proceeded toward the sky. This was followed by one more dream. In that dream, I saw my family members fighting in the darkness below. I was separated from them by light.

At first, I did not understand these dreams. They

seemed wild and nonsensical, out of place, and yet profoundly relevant. As time went by, I believed they were from God, and that he was watching over me. Then, after a while, these dreams somehow started manifesting in reality. This was the beginning of my regaining my strength and confidence.

At this time, I still had no human force to be there for me; there was no one to lend me a shoulder to cry on, no comforting arm or words of wisdom, but what I did now have was the strength and fortitude of God. I believed in Him and, from this profound knowledge, I knew that my self-belief and confidence would be safe. It was a moment of enlightenment, as if something had lifted me by stretching out a hand and rescuing me from the wild and icy turbulence of the churning sea below.

This did not mean that the abuse stopped, but what it did mean was that I had now become a strong young lady. I kept praying and telling myself that the torture I was suffering at this man's hands would, one day, be over.

"I am stronger than this," I would think to myself, even if it was through gritted teeth and clenched lips. By now I was resolute, and reassured myself with solid determination. "I will not try to kill myself again."

From this point, I started to change my mental thinking on how I viewed things; and it is this, I believe, that was the vital turning point. I approached another sister-in-law and some of my nieces and told them about my problems. The difficulty was that no one believed me, or even gave me the time of day to say that everything would be all right. All I could do, after each ordeal of abuse, was to kneel and pray, and whisper to myself, "You will be OK because you are a strong woman."

I had also learned that when I fought the abuser, the consequences were great… and violent. One day when I decided to fight him off me, I found myself locked in a store that was used to keep dog food. I ended up sleeping there, without food or water, for days.

That was the level of suffering I would be subjected to if I so much as dared to protest, to get him away from me. Added to that, anyone else who dared help me would also be severely punished. If my nieces and nephews helped, it meant no food for them, no going to school, being subjected to endless beating and some being raped themselves.

We lived in a beautiful big mansion, and the cars in our compound were to die for: expensive and luxurious. All the other children envied us because, to outsiders, we had everything, we were living the best life. Little did they know that all was not well behind the big gates that guarded the mansion.

I learned to pretend to be obedient – but only whilst I planned the best way out of the situation in which I now found myself. The only option was to run away, but that seemed impossible, as I was locked in the house most of the time, and I had no friends. I could not make friends at school, because of the shame that engulfed me, with what he was doing to me. As a child you internalise this shame, a voice inside tells you it is all your fault. As a result, I remained trapped in an inner turmoil of pain and fear, clothed in blame. Yet, deep inside me, there was another, stronger, voice which kept telling me that I would rise to unimaginable heights, and that I would eventually rise enough to face my fear. At times, this was hard to keep believing, but I did. It was all I had.

At this point, I could not see how rising up to conquer my predicament and become the person I really was could happen, although I continued to play the role of the strong woman inside. That was crucial to my survival. I would go about with my face wreathed in smiles and radiating confidence, which were the tools of disguise, helping me to hide the pain. This was valuable, and helped enormously to power me on. It wasn't perfect but it was a strategy that worked, because it somehow gave me the best way of dealing with my troubled life and being able to face the world. Whenever I smiled at people, they smiled back. Real or not, it did not matter at this point, as I was slowly beginning to get a few people coming closer to me, in spirit and friendship; and this, at least, gave me some sense of relief.

As I began to make friends, I also began to feel more confident about my plan to run away. I knew that if I could make more friends, then I might be able to find someone to take me in to live with them. However, first, I also knew I needed someone to believe me, and the things I would tell them that were happening to me.

What I did know, at that point, was that God was on my side because, as I turned 18, I was sent away to study abroad. This was a happy moment for me, because it meant no more abuse. I was to be away for six years. This consisted of two years of a foundation course, and a four-year degree course. This was the first time I had been away from my home and family, but the only emotion I felt on leaving was relief. Relief at being away from it all.

To me, this was the best thing that could have happened. I was escaping without having to put my plan of running away into action. I gave myself a little smile whilst I waited to board the plane that would take me away and free me from the abuse.

"God does hear prayers," I kept thinking to myself. I had never known the kind of peace and freedom I felt just then.

The plane journey felt like a ticket to heaven. I dreamed of how my life could be improved. I was rigidly determined to work as hard as I could at my studies and be the best that I could because, whatever happened now, I thought, I am not going back home. Ever. God had given me the opportunity, and I was going to use it in every possible way.

The plane landed in a remote town in the south of India. However, after feeling such glorious relief at my escape, I was now in for another shock.

In this new land, the culture was so different from where I had come from. Animals walked freely on the streets, just as they pleased. The roads were congested, owing to animals, cars, motorcycles and all manner of traffic; everyone shared the same road space. The weather was also disturbingly hot. It reached fifty degrees, and would leave you drained and feeling exhausted. Another thing that caused a shock was that the inhabitants in this new land never used toilet paper, sanitary towels or the few other luxuries that I was used to. They could hardly be called luxuries today, more like essentials.

I had a phobia of snakes. Here, snakes were often revered as gods to some of the people. The snakes were everywhere you went, especially in the monsoon season. Monkeys and packs of feral dogs were also a threat.

This was not what I had expected at all, but it was better than what I had been facing at home, and it was worth sticking it out. As the days went by, I discovered more strange customs. I learned how men and women never mixed. In my university, girls would sit on one side of the room and men on the other side. This segregation was the same in every kind of public transport. I soon came to understand that this kind of practice had led to high levels of rape in the country.

This, given my history, was disturbing. I wondered whether I had jumped out of the fat and into the fire, and whether I would be subjected to even worse abuse. The only consolation was that I realised that my racial features would play a role in my protection. I soon learned that the people in this land had a phobia about the colour of my skin. I noticed that no one sat near me. In lessons, the other students would stand in class rather than sit near me. They had never met a person of my type before. My skin colour made me into some sort of alien, from whom they distanced themselves. I also realised that this meant that making friends was going to be an arduous task. However, I was certain that I could survive this. It was less bad than rape and these people, I told myself, simply lacked the knowledge to understand my background or nationality. They did not know any better; or, at least, that is what I told myself.

I got to learn more about their culture. They seemed to be more family-oriented, they valued education and liked children to be doctors, dentists, you name it. High professions.

As time went by I settled in and started my studies. I made a friend or two, found and joined a small Pentecostal church in the region where I was staying. Christians in that region were being persecuted at the time, but I was determined to pray, because faith was all I had. God was my pillar, my rock-solid strength.

This isn't a book that I have written to try to persuade you to follow my faith – or any religion. That may not be what you want, need, or what will help you. What is important, when you are in an extreme situation, as I have been, is identifying the need to find support, in whatever guise that may come: a person, a group or God, but it has to be someone who nourishes you and gives you peace and does not harm your body. I am convinced that this will keep you going, moving along the path of *your* journey, however traumatic or painful it may be.

At this Pentecostal church which I had discovered, I met a tall, handsome young man, who I later came to think of as sent from God. At first sight, he did not appeal to me. I judged him only from the clothes he wore, the way he spoke, and his general demeanour, which I thought were not those of a Christian. He seemed the wrong type for me; but, having met him in church, I decided to give him the benefit of the doubt.

Then, three years into my education, I fell ill. Since the abortion, I had already been experiencing very heavy and painful periods. Although I had experienced heavy periods with clotting, pelvic pain and cramping, during my menstrual periods before, this dysmenorrhoea was far worse than usual. In addition, the pain increased as time went by. The pain would also go on for two weeks after my periods had finished, which meant that I only had another two weeks, at the most, before it began again with the next period. This was accompanied by severe, lower-back pain, which involved my bowel.

As bad as the pain was, I did not want to talk about it because of embarrassment. I associated the condition with the awful abortion which I had had to endure; but unfortunately the pain was not getting any better. Then, as I left lectures one day, I collapsed and was rushed to hospital. I was diagnosed with having a chocolate cyst on my ovaries, which is a cyst filled with old blood, hence the name 'chocolate'. In addition, I had acute appendicitis as they thought, although this turned out to be appendicular endometriosis. The diagnosis was made using a laparoscopy procedure, and led to a series of operations. This involved removal of my appendix and being hospitalised for several months.

Being in a foreign land, I found myself, yet again, in a position of loneliness. There was no one to help me or give emotional support. Once again, I needed to reach into my inner being. I needed to remind myself that I was a strong woman. "If I had survived rape, I could overcome this," I repeatedly told myself – and with a smile on my face.

"Indeed, the smile on your face is your trademark, mother," my daughter told me while she continued to listen to me. "Everyone knows you can bring other people's mood to the most positive, happy place with your smile," and she gently grinned to herself as she listened.

I believed that everything began with a thought. I convinced myself that my thoughts, whatever went on in my head, were what I acted upon. Good or bad. I would therefore think of good things, or things that I believed would make me overcome the situation in which I found myself at the time. I had no money for the hospital, or to pay for food, because in this region the hospitals provided no medication or food without payment. Everything had to be paid for in advance. You even had to pay before an injection was given. It was a pay and receive service. I did not know what I was going to do because I had no money. This was to be the first of six surgeries.

The person who was supposed to support me was my abuser, but once I had arrived in India he stopped sending financial help as a punishment to me for not responding to his messages. I was determined to help myself and not go back to where I had come from. I was under the firm conviction that I could find a solution myself, and I had the strength to ignore him.

4

I was surprised to see the young man whom I had met in church. He came to visit me at the hospital, on the very first day of my hospital stay, after the surgery. He had found out from the head of the church, who had sent an announcement to church members to pray for me. The church leader had been informed by a church member who was staying in the same girls' hostel as me.

I found it odd that this young man had visited me, because he was not really a close friend, and men in that country could be stoned to death if they were seen with women of my race. Interestingly, this young man did not seem to mind about that.

We sat and talked, for the first time on a one-to-one basis. At this point, I was so weak I could barely move. I had just undergone major surgery, losing my appendix in the process. I was in a vulnerable position, and I did not know who else to turn to, so I confided in this young man about my money problems, and the fact that I had no one to whom I could turn, to help me out.

He seemed so easy to talk to, and I just continued talking and talking, in my weakened state. He sat and listened. When I had finished speaking, he looked down at me and stared directly into my eyes.

"What beautiful blue eyes he has," I thought to myself.

He looked so handsome. I had never felt so at ease with anyone in my life. He looked into my eyes and told me the words I will never let go of, the same words that had been playing in my head whenever I prayed.

"Survival comes from your inner strength, knowing who you are and your confidence," he said. "And in most cases, help comes from the most unexpected places."

The following months proved exactly that: help came from the unexpected. He was a person whom I had dismissed at first, but he turned out to be what I needed.

"Knock, knock," he said as he entered my hospital room with his close friend and classmate.

"Who's there?" I would answer.

"Your knight in shining armour, here to rescue and spoil you with today's gifts," he would say.

"Come on in then. I hope you've brought my favourite dish: vegetable fried rice with spare ribs," I said.

"Well, I've brought you more than that. It's the most important meal that everyone should have each day: love, hope and faith. You know I have to remind you that it is a great meal to feed on every day," he said laughing.

"I know, I know, my dear. How is the weather out there? I can't wait to be released out of this cocoon." I wanted to get out of hospital so badly.

We would talk till late. It was like having a piece of strong scaffolding around me, bold and resilient, energising and full of hope, holding me up, giving me the strength to go on. It was just what I needed. It is all anyone needs: just one person who can offer you the support you need. I spent five months in the hospital due to complications, and throughout this time, this pleasant and caring young man came to the hospital every single day. He also brought his friend with him. He brought food and, perhaps the greatest gift of all, he paid for the medication I needed. It was as if he had paid for my survival. He paid for everything I needed to get through recovery and to cope with the rigours of my illness. Otherwise, I'd have been so alone and frightened, until the day of my discharge.

His name was Joel Martin. To me, this man was an angel sent by God. This wasn't simply because he had been there for me and become my emotional and physical rescuer, nor because of him paying for my care; but because after I left the hospital, something strange happened. He vanished. He was simply no longer there, like he had disappeared into thin air, a dust cloud of warm and energising spirit that had wafted away on the wind. I never saw him or his friend again.

The last day I saw this man was when he came to my hostel. He gave me the name and address of the university he was meant to be attending. When I didn't hear from him again, I contacted the university as I wanted so much to find out more about him, especially where he had gone. I discovered that at the time of my being in hospital he had been in his final year of dentistry. Since then he had recently completed his degree and was no longer attending university. I tried to elicit his forwarding details from them, but they would not release his personal contact information to me, citing confidentiality. There was nothing further I could do. I had no further leads. There was no thread I could follow to lead me to him, and I yet felt so indebted to him.

The appreciation for what he had done for me went beyond words. It wasn't just that I felt I owed him a massive debt, or that I felt guilty in any way for taking so much, without the chance to give back. Although I did of course want to give back, it was the simple need to find him that propelled me on in my search, abstract though it was. I knew I would keep trying to find him or his friend; I wouldn't give up easily and forget his support. I would always remember it too.

This is something we call a gift to 'take away with us'. The strength to treasure and remember a source of help. Too often in life we rush on, forgetting the most compelling of human touches, the simplest of voices, the touch of a hand, the person at our side who was there when we needed them most. We rarely ask for these moments of help, and they often arrive when we least expect them. The important element, which is so often overlooked, is the simple recognition that they occurred; more than that, not just being thankful for them but, crucially, going on to strive to be that person to someone else, whether friend, family or stranger.

After my discharge from hospital, I hit another barrier. I could no longer continue with my studies because I was no longer receiving funding for study. The university had no option but to dismiss me. Of course, I wasn't happy about this. I wanted to study and work hard to get a qualification. I wanted, so very much, to put the past and the abuse with which I had been tormented as far away in the past as I could, and move on to a brighter and more positive future. The little I survived on came from charities in the university and distant relatives.

I did all I could to find a solution to the problem of funding, but to no avail. I didn't have the money to pay for the university education, and there seemed to be no viable source from which I could draw, with confidence, to help me. I say 'with confidence', because it was my abuser who was the person who had sent me there. It was not until later that I realised that he did not pay the full tuition fees for the university course. I seemed to be sinking lower with each passing day. Yet it is when you are at your lowest ebb that you can also be at your strongest.

The solution, if you can call it that, was decided for me, and the matter was whisked right out of my hands, leaving me distraught. I was to go back to my home country. It was like an order I could not fight. I had nothing, I had nowhere to go, I was trapped; it was as if, in that moment, I was backed into a corner, being dragged, kicking and screaming, away. This decision to send me back home was breaking me up. It broke my heart in pieces. I did not think those pieces could ever realistically be fixed back together again. The pain cut through me like a sharp, serrated knife. I was certain that the aches which started up in my stomach after this news was received could have been felt by anyone standing within yards of me. Why was this happening? I asked myself again and again. Sometimes, it is best not to ask why.

It was then that the fear, the abuse and all the trauma I had suffered came rushing back, flooding my mind with memory and fear. My blood felt as if fear was rushing around my body. My head was spinning with the confusion of what I should do next. I had to think, and to think fast. My first thought was where I should go, and how I could possibly plan an escape route. Initially, it was about the burning question of where I should go. It loomed up in my mind, large and clear. Going back home, to a life I couldn't face, had not been part of my plan. It felt like going back to face living in a dark corner, from which there would never be any escape. There seemed no way out.

I sat in my hostel room and cried. Large, uncontrollable drops of tears fell. I prayed. "God, if you can hear me," I pleaded, shouting the words out loud, "please, tell me why this is happening."

My mind was in such turmoil, I couldn't think straight. Thoughts of self-harm, and wanting to die, came back to me, haunting me. I did not want to go on. I could not live with myself if I had to go back, if I had to endure again the torture which I thought I had left behind. "This was not the plan, God, not the plan!" were the words I kept repeating out loud.

As night fell and the darkness enfolded around me, I curled myself up into the blanket on my bed and thought of Joel Martin, or Joe as I called him. I remembered the peaceful nature he had, so very calming, and how it was such a joy to be so close to that and to feel its enveloping warmth. I remembered our conversations and the encouraging words he would tell me, willing me to keep going, to fight on. He gave me the reassurance that I would win my fight. I had felt, with Joe by my side, that I could conquer anything. This brought back some strength to me. It wasn't a replacement but, somehow, in the midst of my cascading tears, I managed a smile. I began to think to myself: "Survival comes from within; control your mind, think positive. Just smile and have confidence and face your fears. For only then," I told myself, "will you overcome them." I had to be firm with myself. "Don't, whatever you do, just don't make excuses for yourself, but think of how you can face the challenge. You can face it. You can overcome, and you can win."

These thoughts brought back some light into my mind. To reinforce this, I knelt down and prayed for strength and wisdom.

Landing back in my homeland was the most painful thing I had ever had to endure. It was like going back to a hell from where I had escaped, going back to a life worse than death. I could barely endure the thought, but I also knew that I was armoured with more strength after being away. I was not quite the girl I had been on leaving. Some small spark had changed, but was it enough? I was going back to the same home, the same place where all the abuse had taken place. I would have to face all the people who never cared. They never cared about me or what was happening to me. I might as well have been a discarded piece of rag for all I meant to them, in the pain I was suffering.

I would have to deal with the pretence again, the turning away and ignoring what was going on, how my body was being used. I would have to live again in that terrible environment.

As I stepped off the plane, placing my feet on firm land, I held myself steady. I drew a deep breath, exhaled and stood up straight, like a woman who has never known any fear. This was how I would be, tall and confident, no matter what the trembling inside.

I walked to the terminal building, putting a big, broad smile on my face, and headed for the exit. There was no time now to feel sorry for myself, and I wasn't going to. I was different. I was a new woman. I was no longer the old, terrified, abused victim. The first lesson that I had learned was that confident women have no time to feel sorry for themselves. Pitying yourself makes you lose strength. When you think of yourself in sadness and sorrow, you can almost feel the flow of energy seeping away from you, like water down of an open plughole. I was going to be stronger than that. My biggest test was about to happen.

For the face that greeted me was exactly the face that I did not want to see: my abuser's face. I had not been in contact with him since I had left. I did not know whether he was the same man as he had been back then, and I didn't care. What was important was that I most definitely was not the same girl who had climbed up the steps of that plane, four years before. It was this thought that made me strong, rooting me to the ground and reinforcing my focus.

5

I greeted him with the respect required of me as his junior; a difficult enough task for, in my mind, it was he who was the minor. I lifted my baggage into the car, settled into my seat inside and, from there, it was silence for the entire ride home.

On arrival in my old home, everyone was pleased to see me. They seemed genuinely happy at my arrival. Yet, for all that, all I saw were the same people, wrapped under his arm, in fear. The same fear, the same controlling bully – and bullies are weak.

That first night, I could not sleep. Here I was again. Four years had passed, yet it suddenly seemed as if nothing had changed. I felt my former resolve collapsing. I was trapped again. I was locked in the cage. I was, in his eyes, no different, whatever I might have wanted to feel inside. It was too painful to accept.

As I lay in my bed in a room I shared with my nieces,

I heard the door open very slowly. My heart started to race, a million thoughts went through my head at once. It was late in the evening and everyone was out and about their business. I started praying and asked out loud.

"Who's there?"

There was no answer. I spoke again, but this time much louder.

"Who is there? Please come in." Still there was no answer.

I was in a house full of people, but I could not comprehend why I was so afraid. I got up from the bed and approached the door carefully. I found my niece's eleven-month-old child sitting by the door. I stood there and gazed at her thinking, I was once like this child. My abuser was once like this child. Where did it all go wrong?

"You look lost in thought. Is everything OK?" my niece asked as she picked up her daughter.

"I'm fine, my lovely. I'm just amazed how our little princess has grown."

"They do grow fast, don't they? We're about to catch a movie. Do you want to join us?" my niece asked as she started to walk away.

"No, no, you guys enjoy yourselves. I need some sleep," I replied while trying to stay as positive as possible.

I knew, in that moment, that I had to leave this place as soon as possible. I had no choice. I had tasted freedom and I wanted it back. I was like an animal who has been released into the wild, surviving and thriving and loving the challenge, only to find itself recaptured, imprisoned within a tight, reinforced steel cage… being gawped at and laughed at. At all costs, I had to find my freedom; and this time, I would have to do it on my own. I spent the night planning my escape. I could not sleep. I used every minute available to me. All I knew was that I could not stay another night in that place. I had no idea, no conceivable notion of quite where I was meant to go, but I knew, with absolute conviction, that I had to get out… and fast.

It was now into the second day of my return. As I lay in bed, after a sleepless night, I felt exhausted. It was if I had taken a dramatic step backwards. I felt crushed, like a wounded soldier, too defeated to rise again, knowing that the enemy is just a step away.

My mind began racing. One of the phrases that kept coming back to me was Joel's words that survival comes from inner strength. It would come from all that I had been through and, more significantly, all that I had overcome. I would find a way to run away. I would, and I could. I had to. I had no choice.

As my mind continued to race, I did what I knew would give me the inner courage and strength to carry out my escape. I knelt and prayed. Yes, I did a lot of praying. It was all I had, and it was enough. It was another strength out there to help me, to lessen the loneliness, and to help me to continue treading my path, and not give up or give in.

It was through prayer that it occurred to me to go

back to my mother, whom I had left when I was just four years old. I had only seen her once since then. My father had passed away while I had been abroad. I had not been able to make it back to go to his funeral. This, I decided, was the time to go to see my mother and pay my final respects to my father.

That following morning, I woke and acted as normal. Displaying outward confidence had become a part of me, a robust slice of inner strength, a piece of armour that I could dress myself in, like a protective garment of clothing, and one which belonged to me; it was shaped by me, and it could not be twisted and distorted out of shape. I would not let it.

This was how I joined the family for breakfast. I calmly informed them that I would be going into town for the day, as I had not done so since my return. I got ready and headed straight to the coach station. There was no raising of suspicion. So far, everything was fine. I took nothing with me, apart from the clothes I was wearing, and one change of thin clothing that could fit in my handbag, my passport and the little money that I had left from my hospital help-fund from Joe.

The coach journey was nine, long, frightening hours, each hour taking me further and further away from home, and into the unknown. All I knew was that the unknown ahead would be safer and better than what I had left behind. My biggest fear at this point was that by nightfall they would discover that I was not coming back. Added to this was the curling knot of fear that my abuser was a known man of power. All he would have to do was to make one phone call and I would be caught. My punishment would be swift, ruthless and brutal, leaving no room for explanation, or anything as human as a cry for help. I prayed that I could cross the border before he realised that I had gone.

I was hopeful. It was why I had made an early start. I had already thought out the logistics and, by the time it got dark, I was reasonably sure I would have crossed the border. As these thoughts occupied my mind, filling my head with more urgency, I must have been relaxed as I drifted off to sleep.

I was woken up by a fellow passenger, several hours later; the lady sitting next to me tapped me on the shoulder. "Hey," she said, "we've arrived; you slept almost the entire journey."

"Thank you," I replied. "I needed that nap to stay sane; it's been a tough few days for me." This was said with my usual smile, pasted into place to hide my inner pain.

It was such a relief to have arrived at last. I said a quick prayer and got off the coach. I had no idea what lay ahead of me, but what I did know was that anything was better than what I had left behind. I had, at least, a small bite of freedom.

I duly arrived at my mother's home sometime after midnight. It had been nineteen long years since I had seen her. I was never allowed to go and visit my parents. My brother already knew that having endured so much abuse in living with him, there was no way he was going to send me to see my parents. I am sure he would have suspected that I would speak out, and this is my view to this day of why he never sent me back to Botswana to visit them. He was scared of what my mother would think, because she trusted him to take care of me. I had grown up and I had grown stronger. I now returned as a confident twenty-two-year-old woman.

My mother was so happy to see me. She was an old lady by now, but full of energy. We both cried and talked all night, but not once did I trouble my mother with what had transpired over the years. I knew that this was my burden to carry. As the night progressed, my mother realised that I had arrived with no belongings.

"Oh, my child," she said. "I haven't seen you in so many years, and you come for a day?" She spoke with the same happy grin still on her face.

"No, mother," I responded, "I am here to stay for a few days."

"But you have no luggage?"

"I was robbed of all my things on the way," I lied, "because of travelling so late."

At this point in my life, I knew I would find a way through anything that life threw at me. I was often not aware of it, but my head was constantly running to find solutions to looming problems, fears and barriers.

Village life was not at all easy to get used to, because of the lack of modern facilities. The serenity in the place was something else, and it was worth giving up a few of life's basic luxuries for more spartan living; it was so peaceful, with the beautiful sunny mornings, and the birds up with the dawn light, singing. The place was unbelievably peaceful. All you could see for miles was green scenery, and all the foods were fresh and natural. There was no fridge, no electricity and not even an indoor toilet. I found it extremely difficult not being able to go to the toilet at night, because outside was pure darkness and it was almost impossible to find. This was very hard to get used to.

I spent the first few days visiting relatives and enjoying being a visitor in this new, tranquil place, where I could allow myself to blend in with the surroundings. As time went by, reality started to sink in. I needed to find a way forward. Living here in this remote village couldn't be what I needed, as I had already seen too much of the world to be able to settle here. I did not need to be convinced, I knew it.

My mother started to see my distress. "I may be old," she said to me one day, "but I am still wise." She gave me a long, hard look. "I can see that you are troubled," she went on, "please, speak to me."

"I don't have anything to go back to, mother," I replied. "At this moment, I don't know what to do with my life."

Another lesson I had learned about confidence was to have no fear in asking for help when it was needed. Having had no support through my earlier troubles, it had taught me to admit when I needed help.

My mother studied my features. "Go back to the city where you belong; what you need to do with your life will come to you."

I looked at her and listened.

"I will raise some money to get you started," she said.

After I'd stayed for some time in the village, my mother had raised enough money to get me back to the city.

I went to stay with my mother's friend in the city while I continued to look for a way forward. Without possessing any certificates to prove my education, I couldn't get a job. The first thing I began to aim for was to get a visa so that I could go abroad. I had what might best be described as an American dream. I had no money and no job, and possessed little else other than the clothes which I stood up in, and yet I had this confidence that I could get to the dream land, wherever that was. I would find my way; I would somehow get there.

I pursued the process required to apply for a visa, day and night, but to no avail. I had to leave and go somewhere far away; it was my only course of action. I had to get away, and I couldn't risk my abuser coming after me. I met several individuals who could make this happen, but the problem was that they all asked for favours which I could not give. As much as I was desperate, I would not give in to bribery. Lesson number three, I had learned as a confident woman, was to stay strong and be able to say 'no' to situations and requests that came my way, without feeling guilty.

My friend's mother got to the point where she could not keep me anymore. She gave me a week to find a solution to my problem. Most of the help I found came from men, but having suffered so much abuse from a male, every man was a potential abuser in my eyes.

It was, of course, a barrier for me. I believed that every man who wanted to help me only offered to do so because he wanted to gain sexual favours and abuse me. I know this may not sound fair on all the good and kind men who are out there, but it was a result of what had happened to me. I knew no other life.

However, I was strong enough to confront this. I knew that, at some point, I was going to have to pull my survival strength out of the bag, rise up in confidence and face my fears again.

During that same week, my mother's friend had a male friend come to visit from Switzerland. He had a good position in a university, and he could help me to get sponsorship. This was my chance, I thought. Such offers don't come along like that too often, and need to be snatched up when they do. I couldn't afford to lose it. I had to gather my strength and approach this man for help to get me a visa. He was intrigued by the level of confidence and determination I portrayed. Girls of my age would not usually approach older adults of his standing in the way that I was doing. I was emboldened. I knew that if I did not seize this chance, I would later come to regret it.

"So I understand you want to come to Switzerland?" he said, looking at me with a serious scary face.

"Yes, sir."

"What is your passion? What would you like to study?" he asked.

"Law or biochemistry, sir."

"Do you always give such short answers? If this was an interview, I would not be impressed. You have to sell yourself. And don't call me sir," he continued. "Just call me Uncle Dennis."

He then looked at me as if to see my reaction to his comments. Then he turned and looked at my mother, who was also there at the time, and said, "Are you going to contribute to this conversation?"

"Not really," she said without looking at him, but with her eyes on me.

"Hmm," he said.

"My daughter can speak for herself. She is shy and reserved, but trust me, she can handle you," my mother said with a broad smile on her face.

"Well then, Miss Sunshine, law or biochemistry?"

I thought about it carefully. I wanted either to do law or be a doctor. I wanted to defend people or treat people.

"Biochemistry," I said.

To my amazement, he agreed to help, and enrolled me into his university… but on one condition. I would have to pay for my college fees and accommodation myself. At least he hadn't asked me for sexual favours. However, it was a barrier. Once again, I did not know how or where the money would come from, but I readily accepted. The visa process started up and went into full swing. The man offered to pay for my visa fees, which he said he would need to have repaid to him once he was back in Switzerland.

God was with me. I went for the interview, and the interviewer did not ask any questions. On the same day as the interview, I was granted the visa. All I could do was kneel and pray and thank God. Truly believing in yourself and in your confidence can take you a long way. This made me even stronger. I now fully believed that I could get even further.

After that, my mother and her friend bought me a ticket to Switzerland. I had nowhere to stay when I arrived there. Fortunately, I had a sister-in-law who took me in.

Switzerland is a country in central Europe, a beautiful place known for its famous cheese and Swiss chocolates. It is a beautiful country with its great outdoors. It was a completely different experience to when I landed in Asia, although there are some commonalities. I arrived in the middle of winter. Having come from the sun of Africa, the winter seemed harsh, even though to the locals it was good weather at the time. I quickly had to adapt and enjoy the civilisation of Europe. First was the simple greeting with a handshake, as opposed to the African kneeling to greet or the Asian bow or a nod. There is difference in food too: in Africa most food is organic; in Europe there is a lot of frozen foods, but what I loved about Switzerland is that they did not eat a lot of fast food. Sadly, there were no beautiful sandy beaches as in Asia; instead, one settled for the freezing snow.

"Welcome to Europe," my sister-in-law said as we drove through the snow to her apartment.

I did not answer. I just sat with my head on the window, staring at the falling snow and taking in the beauty of this lovely country. It was unimaginable to think of how differently people lived; how one place could be so hot yet another so cold at the same time. The architecture was just breath-taking. I drifted back to Africa, to the girls still trapped in a life of torture and abuse. I would have to work hard; I would have to help them, is all I could think.

The journey was not long: just 45 minutes' drive from the airport to her apartment, which was a truly beautiful place. The view of the park and the ponds: I had never seen trees without leaves. Where I was from, it would get cold but trees would still have leaves. Minor things, yet so different from what I knew. Switzerland in general had homes finished to high standards. I easily felt at home.

I enrolled at university, where I would later obtain my degree. To cover the cost of the fees, I worked in a nursing home, and I also worked as a maid for my sister-in-law, to cover my rent. I toured Bern, the capital, whenever I could. The people were not as friendly as in Africa, but I was used to being alone so I did not interact with many, and I was limited to English-speaking people.

Juggling everything was not easy, but success usually requires hard work, and I was determined not to fail. Illness had been such a hindering factor before. This time round, my success depended on me. I had no one on whom I could rely, whether financially, emotionally or for anything else. I only had myself, and I knew that I would need to work very hard.

6

Earning my university fees and my keep by myself brought me a feeling of inner confidence. I was self-reliant, no longer leaning on someone else or under their control to become educated and go further in life. It was hard work, but it was freedom. It gave me the beginning of what was to become a solid, coping mechanism.

Then, in the continuing process of trying to heal, I came across other individuals who had also suffered abuse. When you have suffered something traumatic, you often try to find people who have been through what you have gone through, or something similar, by reading self-help forums or joining groups. You think they will understand you, but we all cope in different ways; I found that people of my ethnic background did not talk so freely about such matters, whereas Europeans were more liberal, which helped a great deal in my healing process.

One of the things I learned, as I met and engaged with others, was that when you have suffered abuse, you may become one of three things. You might turn into an abuser yourself, by bullying others; you might try to be a saviour, by saving everyone around you who has been through a similar experience; or you might become a pioneer, trying to stand up to injustice.

Turning into any one of these three personalities has its dangers. If the aftermath of being abused is not approached carefully, it can lead to a different sort of turmoil. The problem is that you may find yourself losing a lot of good relationships, simply because of not knowing where to draw the line. Remember, you can never equate exactly your own experience and inner thinking with that of someone else. Another person may have come through an ordeal scarred in a very different way, and reacting quite differently, with a mindset that isn't an exact match to your own. The actions which they take will be dependent on their thinking and whatever influence they have absorbed along their path, just as you will have taken on your own thinking and adjustments.

The choice of who I became largely depended on those around me. The major factor was always how I controlled my mental state. This is the only thing in your life over which you can have absolute control. It governs your every move. You choose what to do in life, and in which direction to turn. You and no one else. Knowing and understanding this concept can give you enormous strength. It is realising that the most precious and vital tools in life, which can take you a long way, are free.

Moving on, something unexpected occurred. Two years into my education, I started to suffer debilitating health problems. The same condition which I had suffered before had come back to strike me again. It started as the same condition but now developed into something more serious, a worse form of endometriosis. It was discovered that all my pelvic organs were stuck together, involving the bowel, and I therefore had to undergo another operation, to have these separated, as well as to remove the endometriosis.

I was so very alone in my soul now; there was no one close to me to whom I could turn and lean on for support. I had never known the love of a mother; I had been raped by a family member. I became pregnant through this and was taken off to have an illegal abortion performed on me, which I believe led to the endometriosis, the condition that was now giving me grief.

This was all a massive further blow, and it interrupted my studies. I had by now moved out of my sister-in-law's home, and I was sharing a flat with my university mates. They were good to me, and looked after me during my recuperation process. I steadily recovered, although not fully. I was feeling just like Joseph in the Bible: abandoned by my family and at the mercy of strangers. It seemed that this was happening on every level, but somehow or other I found a way to survive.

I continued to suffer pain, on and off, but through my ordeal, and in resuming my studies, I would regularly pray. I would strive to find the prayers to keep me going and give me the inner strength I needed. It helped to enable me to maintain my outer mask, of playing confident with a broad smile, to keep me going. I continued to study at home as much as I possibly could, determined not to fail. Eventually, I managed to sit my final university exams. To my relief and joy, I passed with a 2.2 honours degree in biochemistry. My hard work had paid off. This was success indeed.

Coming out of university, I managed to secure a job in my field of study, but my health problems had not gone away. Something else now happened. During a routine smear test, the clinicians discovered that there were unexpected, and abnormal, changes in the cells of my cervix. In effect, this meant the beginning of cervical cancer. Combined with my endometriosis, this gave me endless pain. I felt certain that there was another factor that had caused this condition. I was sure the abortion I had endured had brought this on.

I began to search for the causes of endometriosis. This is a condition in which tissue that reacts like the lining of the womb is found in other parts of the body. It is thought that one of the possible causes of the condition is retrograde menstruation, where some of the lining flows up through the fallopian tubes, rather than leaving the body. I became convinced that the abortion I had, which had been brutal and mismanaged by an amateur person, had gone wrong and caused this condition in me. However, I had no proof.

The doctors agreed with me that this could be a possible cause of the endometriosis, but it was not possible scientifically to prove it. Not knowing what the future would bring for me, I had to make a big and tough decision. To be free of the pain, I would have to accept removal of my womb and cervix. I thought about this long and hard. This meant losing all hope of ever having the children which I could have had in the future. In weighing up all circumstances, I knew that removal of my womb was the best choice for me, if I were to have a chance of living a pain-free life, even though I knew that this was not guaranteed. Doctors told me that the condition could come back, so long as a woman's ovaries are still intact, as a few cells can be missed. I had, in total, six surgical operations, the last one leading to me developing severe sepsis, and I underwent an early menopause too because they finally removed the ovaries.

At this time, I was also undergoing a citizenship process, as I had applied for permanent residence. The underlying issue here was that I knew there was a possibility that I could be refused and returned to my birth country. Going back and facing my past all over again was not something I could countenance. The thought weighed heavily upon me. I longed for peace of mind, for the feeling of inner calm and the freedom, in every sense, which accompanies that; in mind, body and spirit.

Since I had met Joel, I had never told anyone else about my traumatic ordeal. Now, I longed for that ability to share and unload. I longed for someone to talk to. I wished, day and night, for someone to be there, who wouldn't judge me, someone who wouldn't feel sorry for me either, but who would, instead, stand by my side and simply listen and tell me that everything would be OK. These thoughts, I knew in my soul, were for the weak. That wasn't me. I would immediately snap out of these thoughts, smile and move on my way.

I realised, too, that smiling took me to another place. When I smiled, I no longer felt sad or depleted, and my smile touched people. I started smiling as often as I could.

The surgery went well, and I had no regrets at what had been performed with the removal of my womb, but the recovery process was not easy. Because of the constant on-and-off pain, I missed work so often that it eventually led to my dismissal. I had no choice but to let go of my job and look for work through an agency. This meant working when I could, and taking on simpler administrative roles which were not strenuous. This went on for a long period of time.

Another problem now loomed. I had taken a lot of time off work, and had not been able to keep up to date with new developments. By the time I felt fully recovered, I was unable to use my degree unless I went back to study for another year. I did not have the money to fund this, so I had to settle for the smaller administrative jobs. Although these covered my bills, life was difficult. I had incurred so many debts during my recovery process, and I needed to progress with my life. I had to find something to do to increase my income. In the meantime, I continued with my roles as an administrator.

I met many high-profile people in this position. I used my confidence to fit in, as I slowly worked my way up. I would dress in clothes that were equivalent to their level, even though they had millions and I had nothing. I carried myself with such confidence and grace that I commanded a room full of people. Only those close to me knew that I would go a week just having bread and tea. I lost so much weight but, because I never showed any weakness, everything seemed fine and wonderful in the eyes of others. The more broke I was, the more they commended me, complimenting me on how great I looked. I knew it was God who had given me this prize. The God who had protected me from such a young age, and who would always be with me.

However, things worsened for me. I couldn't go on like this. I needed money and I needed it fast. I asked my usual friends whether they could help me, but every single one of them responded that they did not have the means to help me. This is when I knew my strength was required the most.

I knew then that I needed to do something that I had never done before. I needed some form of income that didn't require too much struggle. I prayed to God for a way through. I felt so low, so utterly forlorn and lost. I distanced myself from my family and friends. I switched my phone off and sat in my flat, thinking of how I was going to deal with all the debt I had acquired. As I sat in my home and gave increasing thought to this, penniless and alone, I began to write. Before long, I was writing down the story of my life. I did not know what would come out of this, but I knew that I had to try to do something unusual. I had to step outside my comfort zone.

It took me the whole weekend to write my story. Sad as it was to recall the events and the trauma of what had happened to me, I also felt a rising happiness at writing it all down. I was fearful that it would all sound so depressingly sad that no one would get beyond the first chapter. This was only the first step, though. Next, I would need to get the book published.

Publishing the book was another story. I did not know where to start, and the language I had used was not convincing enough to sell. I started looking for an author to edit my draft. Courage was required to approach top writers. They can dismiss you like worthless worms, if your material is not worth their time. The writer I eventually contacted was a top writer, with bestsellers to his name; and because I had no money to pay the writer, it meant convincing him to take a risk on me, and on a short story that came from a non-celebrity, because he only co-wrote for top clients. To my astonishment, he agreed and had a look at my story. He liked it and agreed to edit it, for an agreement on profits.

The book went into production and was published. It immediately became a hit – far more than I thought it would. It sold a good number of copies in its first few months. I could not believe it, I had broken free.

With my first pay cheque I made investments, to make sure I was financially secure. I continued to work in my administration job for several years afterwards. With the money I earned, I built a small school and a shelter to take in and counsel young abused children, as well as to educate girls on endometriosis. Life looked good. I have since taught young women how to be confident and learn that rape and daily troubles cannot hold you down, if you remain strong and are confident. Above all, you must change your mindset, because all actions start in the mind. My approach has been a huge success.

By now tears were flowing down my daughter's face. I could not tell whether they were tears of sadness or relief. She sat there silently just gazing at me. Her face had mixed emotions.

My daughter is the queen of hugs and I could tell that at that moment, she was giving me one of her tight hugs.

I didn't know if I should continue or stop. My daughter is a free spirit and has the most caring heart. I wanted her to be alright, I wanted her to say something so I know how she was feeling. I wondered what was going on in her mind. I wanted her to learn from my story but not be bitter towards anyone in any away. I wanted to teach her to have a strong mind and for her heart not to harden. I wanted to see the value of her mind and not have it tormented by my story. I decided to stop for a moment and let her compose herself and see if I can interpret her emotion and, better still, ask how she felt.

"That can't be it," she said in astonishment as I stood up to go make us some refreshments.

"You still have not told me how you met Dad."

"I will do so in a moment my dear, let me make us a quick drink to quench our thirst."

"I will do it mother," she said getting up, wiping tears off her face. "You sit tight and relax, you deserve to be spoilt right now," she said with a grin appearing on her teary face. Seeing that grin made me realise that she was in a good place.

As she walked away, I sat back down, took a moment to reflect on how powerful it felt to be able to narrate my own story without shedding a tear. It was a good feeling. It was like a new realisation of what I had known all along. I was FREE.

My daughter came back with her hands full. She had a tray full of treats and a portable Bluetooth speaker.

"Here's to us, I thought a classical tune in the background to lighten the mood would be great," she said.

"I agree," I replied candidly while I poured us some drinks and she popped on her Bluetooth to start the music. Music in our home was life. We enjoyed singing and listening to all sorts of music.

We sat and enjoyed our drink for a moment before I continued.

Following on from this success, financially everything fell into place, but I still felt so lonely. I had struggled to form relationships, because of my history of abuse and distrust of all men. As I could not have children, this also interfered with my life. Most of the men who approached me were young and with no children. I would instantly draw away from them, because I felt they deserved more. They needed to meet a girl who could give them a family. Then, one night, when I was at a party with friends, I met a young man. He was ten years younger than me, which made things worse. As usual, I tried to push him away, but he persisted.

"Hello," I answered the phone to the unknown caller.

"Hello, Joyful," he said with cheesy grin in his voice.

"Long time no see. I thought I should touch base to see how you're doing," he said.

"May I ask who this is?" I did not recognise the name and voice.

"It's Boss." He joked because that was not his name, but it was the nickname I called him the night I met him. "I thought I should touch base and see how you're doing."

"Ooh, how on earth did you get my number? Sorry, let me rephrase that, why on earth did Ann give you my number? I know you must have got it from her. She is the only person we have in common."

"She did you a favour," he said, laughing. "Tell me you're not happy to hear from me." He chuckled.

"You're so full of yourself," I said. "I've already told you, I have so many issues and I'm too old for you. What do you really want?"

"Nothing, just to get to know you. I find you fascinating. I found you funny. I'm just attracted to you. Is that so wrong, just because you're a few years older, which you don't even look? Let's make a deal: I will take you out to dinner three times, and if any one comes up to us and says you are my mother, then I'll leave you alone."

That was how we started. We spoke for a long time that night. He asked where I was from, we joked about me telling him that I could be his mother the night we met, and so on. It was a beautiful moment.

We ended up getting together, and had a sexual relationship, knowing there was no more that could come from this. I could not allow this to spiral into anything too serious and produce children, as I could not have any children. We agreed to have no strings attached. I thought, as time passed, he would realise that I was not for him; he would see that he had made a mistake.

What I did not realise is that I was trying to make decisions for him about his feelings for me. This is a mistake so many of us make. How do you know what someone else is thinking? How could I know what was in his heart? This is how we push away people who try to love and care for us. The trauma you go through can blind you. You start thinking negatively and believe everyone thinks the way you think.

Mindset: yes, I decided to approach the relationship with a different mindset. I decided to set the standards of what I wanted and let him know what I would not compromise on because I believed in being open. Many relationships fail because many go into relationships with a baggage from the past. They do not discuss these things at the start so that you can take up knowing all of each other. I stopped making decisions about me for him, and rather enjoyed the moment. I would let him be as long as we were happy and he was treating me right and he knew all there was to know about me. In the process, I would also ask everything I wanted to know. We formed a really good friendship.

Three years passed, and he was still there, we were still together. As time went on, he began to treat me more as a potential life partner, instead of a friendly sexual partner. I, too, started giving in to him, and eventually decided to give him a chance. This young man knew my problems, and if he had stayed around for this long, then I began to think he must really care about me. We started going out seriously and married a year later. A year into the marriage, we adopted our only child, you, my dear Grace.

You mean a lot to us. You are everything we could have dreamed of. I felt that my life was now where it should be. I was a successful businesswoman, with a loving husband and the most loving daughter. I could only give thanks to God, because he had been my saviour throughout, a force of strength.

There are things that my husband doesn't know about, of all the terrible things that happened to me in the past. I wanted to tell him, but he said my past didn't matter to him and, quite frankly, his did not matter to me either. It was here and now that was important. What we had was too special to be ruined by anything from the past.

I say to anyone to be confident; combine it with your inner strength, and always set your mind to the positive, to help you survive. Never lose who you are, for the sake of success; you may stand alone, but not once will you be alone. God is always watching over you. Most importantly, everything you go through can make you stronger, because each struggle you overcome shows you that you can handle more than you think possible. Always view every problem as a life hurdle that you need to jump, a challenge for you to get through; sometimes it may feel like you are climbing through a hoop, surrounded by fire, but you can come through, even if you are a little bruised and battered; you can survive and win. With practice, you learn how best to jump through the hoops to get to the next one. Never, ever, feel sorry for yourself; that is the greatest barrier next to fear. It compounds fear and inhibits your action. I found my success after 40 years, and I have never looked back. Looking back can turn you into a pillar of salt. Remember the eyes are at the front, not the back.

My only regret is that I have never managed to find Joel, even with all of modern technology. He was an angel, and one whom I wish I could personally greet and thank.

Throughout all this, I had no family to lean on, but I did meet some wonderful people. You may be alone, but if you develop a strong mind and just one good person to support you, then you can survive.

www.ingramcontent.com/pod-product-compliance
Lightning Source LLC
Chambersburg PA
CBHW071706030726
47592CB00014B/2723